Love
Letter
to an
Afterlife

Love Letter to an Afterlife

Ines P. Rivera Prosdocimi

Black Lawrence Press

Black
Lawrence
Press

www.blacklawrence.com

Executive Editor: Diane Goettel
Book and Cover Design: Amy Freels
Cover art: "The joy at the pool" by Miguel Hernandez

Copyright © 2018 Ines P. Rivera Prosdocimi
ISBN: 978-1-62557-803-7

Published 2018 by Black Lawrence Press.
Printed in the United States.

For My Family, Mi Familia, La Flia

CONTENTS

The Lost Santos

I.
Every summer, as a child, I am sent to you, Tía.
And though I have no santos, I love yours.
When the power goes out shadows walk
beneath an oil lamp's burn; copper silhouettes cut air,
and your stories wake the women watchers of night.
Plump hands press against me, so I listen
to your singing, to a song from across the Atlantic.
Arms rock me, as you stuff women into my mouth.
I drink spirits you pour into me; the rocking chair creaks
beneath the weight of my tiny body wrapped
in the white nightgown embroidered with my name.
Blessings, I ask. Bendición, you echo.

II.
Our house is a home full of women.
Full of honey and purple scarves to wrap thick hair in.
Full of strings we attach to each other's toes and tug
when we are too weak to rise in the dark.
Full of water and old Cuban boleros so the moon
remains forever like the rooster's dried foot.
My aunt talks into the night. The women watchers rise
from under the ground. We brush each other's wool hair,
singing to santos overshadowing pictures of our dead.
Hidden in closets, the faces of my relatives
peer up at Saint Michael's foot—the tip of his sword
a silver point pointing down at the earth.

III.
The women in my family whisper from within altars
my aunt built, next to the santos she believed watched
over us. I go to them now, blowing candles out,
poking at powder crosses covering the floor.
And though I drink the water from the Rose of Jericho,
and eat the flowers blooming at night, they disappear
when I place my aunt's picture beside them.

But at night I hear my Tía's voice, and sing.
I sing even though oil lamps don't burn: the santos have left.
Our house is bare except for altars I wipe clean,
and the sound of water moving around my feet.

Communion

I am eight.
Facing la Catedral Primada,

my digits out in front of me,
launching birds into shadows

the palm trees cast;
the color of God's face.

A woman nearby curses
sins out of her head.

Leave my birds alone, or else
I'll kill you

with my thoughts.
My shadow, skinny and long,

lifts his penny loafer to stomp
on birds I cast her way.

I try to punch my shadow flat,
like boxers I've watched

in the TV box souls get stuck in.
But it's safer here then

in the cathedral bells.
I'm going to be a bird doctor

when Mama's shoes fit.
I'll peel back the ears of ivory corn

like she showed me, throw kernels
here, in this field that's a coral cage.

Mama's going to come live here.
My sis & all of my friends.

But there's a woman divining
my future, reading sins

in her hands. She knows
what I hide inside.

Shut my eyes. Mute the mumbling.
I peak through my fingers, see white

trees with monster feet grow all around
& a boy who tells me to climb.

Up I go, behind him,
to find glass lizards

hiding & if I eat the wafer
waiting, today, it will be sweet mango

I've stolen to stuff myself with,
and give to the boy

whose prayers I bump against,
inside his mouth,

to save us. Birds grow
seven colossal wings each.

Build my dreams far away
from the cathedral bells,

they say, I'm like them. One day
peacock feathers will grow from my back,

& an extra pair of eyes
for the daggers thrown my way.

They Say the Santos Sang Through You

for Josefa Rivera Rincón

A white room with white curtains, white walls.

White tiled floor. The white sheets,

crisp and clean, flat across the bed.

You lie there, looking up at the ceiling.

The white footsies to cover my steps.

You mumble something about a missing glass

or a song misplaced. I touch you

with white gloves. So quiet.

The nurse's white uniform. White tray

beside your bed. Your white medical bracelet

there. It hurts your wrist, you say.

Your black skin against all that white.

You still look so pale.

Your white nightgown. Your white sweater.

The island heat does not smother you.

You call me by my aunt's name,

move your eyes across the ceiling, back again.

The white crescent moons of your nails.

Your hands telling me your pocket book

disappeared, asking where is your sister?

The whites of your eyes, small and smaller,

as you squint to take a better look at me.

And you call my name. *Morena,* you say.

The white of your teeth when you smile.

The white of your teeth when you sing:

Under the water, I'll live. I live, counting the waves.

The Girl Who Taught Me to Scream

For the first time my mother left me—
sitting in Montessori, in safety
of the reading area. I remember
feeling minutes or seconds spread
when I wanted nothing but to crawl
inside my mother. *Charlotte,* they spat.
Charlotte colored walls, the floor, desks.
She came to me, startling. Her red hair
cropped above her eyes. She planted a kiss
atop my head, drew her way into
my hand, and led a crayon across
my palm. How swift she was forced
onto her feet. And stumbled. I looked
for my mother for Charlotte locked
in the map room, as her big, amber eyes
bore into mine, as she pressed her nose
against the glass, as her heart-lips blew
a kiss for me, smiled a toothed smile.
Screamed. Later, she circled the room.
A game of duck duck goose. She eyed
the giant maps hung on giant spools,
and climbed a flattened globe. I saw her
hands clutch a canyon. Knees buckle.
The jagged stars along her sneakers.
Her hair rising like fire.

Two Trees

Two trees inside me.
The Flamboyan's red petals. The Aromo's yellow buds.
Their arms rub as I open my mouth.
I've got la güira scraping my throat,
El bandoneón blowing out my chest, and roads
Marking my place at the center of this body
Split into two countries. Roads. El Conde's amber
Cobblestones, where Columbus's door is sealed shut.
And Corrientes Avenue, its hundreds of books
An old philosopher tells me to put down.

Home is a numbered house, cross on the ground,
A country whose balconies I've tight-roped,
Where I have worn a crown of flowers
Lopsided on my head, and announced I was queen.
I have slept in mausoleums, felt people I couldn't touch,
Nor hold in the earth between my thumb and index finger,
In the Ozama river, in El Tigre, whose currents sing
Boleros, Milongas. I play on a piano. My home is:
A pear-shaped flag, underneath my ribcage.

The Mirage

Mama says in you, one day, I'll rest.

Woman, your indigo dress: skin of cotton.

I search for santos in the landscape of your moons.

You move, sashaying to a tune in your head.

The ocean break. My ear against you–

God. The sway of your everything glides by.

Taunt me with the black pearls you hold up.

You are soft, wet dirt, something to mold.

I tell Mama how each day you come like a song

I think I've heard. She warns me never to touch you,

unless to enter the devil's mouth.

How you make sun and shadow one.

I am six, praying to the invisible imprint

your hand has left across my face.

My Barrio

I.

From behind blue gates, Ensanche Luperon simmers: roosters flap against crisscross bars, howling at the Dominican sun; metal blinds open their eyelids and silhouettes slide behind them; vendors pedal over loose rocks and uneven asphalt, yelling goods they've handpicked, as keys jingle in lock after lock. El barrio rises to a sticky heat and breeze muting music seething out from car windows, conversations emanating from every pastel-colored home. Salt and dust lick the sweat between my joints, between my knuckles, behind my legs, the inside of my arms, the back of my neck. I grab a glass bottle from beneath the sink, wanting to go to the corner *colmado* and exchange it for a new one. But see I've never been able to smile at the neighborhood boys, their *pisst pisst* make my walk fall awkward and unsure beside my girlfriends' strut. The sway of their hips. Like merengue is stuck between their thighs. So *pa'lante* I don't go. I sit, sketchbook on my lap, all morning saying, *Buenas* to Ensanche Luperon.

II.

Afternoons settle like the sigh from a lung. Everyone has showered morning off. We sit with the smell of papayas and milk, with the tiny saffron flower heads scattered beneath our brown feet, as boys swing sticks, girls dodge rubber balls. Chairs tilt back after the Flamboyans reach up and across the sky; their slender arms extend down the length of the street to knock on El Loco's door. Time to beg for the fix he first met in Nueva York. *Doña Josefaaa Josefaaa!* His howl crawls through the house walls like something scurrying and afraid. My aunt places the same silver coin in his hand. My silence is a question asking if he'll ever stop chasing. She gives me the same silver answer: *Buenooooooo, Si dios quiera.* I imagine God laying its hand on El Loco's matted hair, the touch straightening his teeth and tongue, so he can be understood among the living, and I can ask him what he went searching for in the big city—ask if it ever promised something like Ensanche Luperon.

III.

Evening. I smack dominos down with my best friend Julian, who says: Listen. *Esas una bachata*. The sound runs high-pitched; fingers staccato over the steel string of a guitar, illuminating us more than the *luz* Julian stole from another house lights his game. And that's when everyone arrives:

La Araña, his night-black skin shining as he squints for the glasses he's never had.

Raquel and Fidelina, hand in hand, armed with fight and belly-full laughter.

Famalie's sweet, *Hola Mi'amor*, a ring of talcum protecting her neck.

Miguel Angel, *El Salsero*, asking, *Que lo que?* as he steps up to the game.

Richard, *El Pelotero*, pitching glove under his arm, knuckles cracked for combat.

Pochi's boulder-belly bounces as his *chancletas* pound the floor.

Alfie tripping on her walk because she always hears her father's call.

Jonathan, *El Chino*, spitting talk at the girls with *tigeraje*. One eye on the game.

My brother Michel. My sister Patricia: duo dressed for the club, but *ni fu ni fa*, stuck at home because Hernan, blue eyes on the block, couldn't get his dad's ride.

And it's no game without Maurico, his clunk-a-junk for a car, screeching to a stop, his laugh provoking a new game. That's when we really start smacking our dominos down, and voices from the radio ring as loud as loud as *Aye! Mi Madre!*

One flat piece follows another, all the size of a thumb, laid out like tiny bodies trying to spell something out. We calculate the weight in our hands, counting each pip on the face of each piece left. Slowly, we build a chain that remembers moves we've made.

When rum sits warm in our bellies, our pieces lay flat in a labyrinth of math. We tell jokes until dawn while making paper plate clothes for the street kittens we want. And one by one, say goodbye, telling each other, *No' chequeamos*, music still reverberating in our ears. Ensanche Luperon opening its arms up as each one of us walk down its street. Home.

IV.

Ensanche Luperon *te amo*. More profoundly than the love I know in English. And when I return to your house, #49, and pack the portrait of my father in my suitcase, off to the USA, I will be taking you, every being on your face, every animal that limps in your hair, all the flowers from behind your ears, the curve of your lips and your big white teeth telling me to laugh, laugh without hesitation. This face marks a spot where I am from.

I leave you my game.

May it break down gates and crush walls crowned in broken glass. May it lay down guns that pop at night. May it dull knives used to pick locks and scissor through strings holding buttons in place. May it remember how the machete cuts cane, not flesh.

I trust that it will echo your name and bring the music we've sung.

Elementary Education

South Carolina. I was six years old,
fought my brothers, blasting

booger balls & laser beam stares.
The only monument: A firecracker stand,

by the hotel that did not let us in.
My souvenir: The Hornets' Nest.

I played with its fuse, wanting bees
to shoot out & drop like grenades.

The raccoons on the roadside,
reminded me of the tooth fairy,

Rat Perez, living in our Magnolia.
I counted my teeth at the motel;

its smell of moth balls & mold
the morning we left for the big building

Mama was going to teach in.
My parents had told me:

One day you'll get a college degree,
then a Masters, then . . .

That building's halls were long & wide
soccer fields. There were closets

where my voice came back to me,
portals I could enter & hide

from the alligators I saw at night.
That building had a real round man;

his bald head all shine & slick,
when he asked, *Your* children?

looking Papa up and down.
Ours.

We drove home at night.
No one said nothing.

A beam of light from a passing car
hit my Mama's pale face,

the back of Papa's hand, dark against her cheek
he caressed. I remembered a boy from school

asking me why I didn't look like my parents.
I understood the question, right there,

in the backseat & wondered if the tooth fairy
could change our colors in exchange for a tooth.

Playing Rocky and Apollo

Our boxing gloves were tube socks.
wrapped round our knuckles;
cotton cushions we slapped and bumped
like professionals. My sister and I marched,
locking eyes with our corner men.

Our brothers smeared Vaseline
across our faces, shoved mouth guards
in our mouths. They built us up,
saying things like, *Slip the jab. No fear.*

She kept her arms tucked against her ribs.
Gloves up. Chin down.
Eyes fixed to spot an opening.
Silently, her fist cut the air.

A snapping inside my body,
a subtle shifting of weight.
And I rode the punch.
Limbs and tendons: A calculation
of force absorption.

Our bodies: one giant muscle
contracting, then expanding,
a war inside the ring,
amongst the twin beds we slept in,
matching floral comforters,
Bob Marley and Michael Jackson posters,
the giant red reading chair.

We punched out of that animal clinch,
craving our one minute sanctuaries.
Then the dance began again, and I remembered
a cockfight we'd watched in horror.
They never end until one rooster quits.

Miguel's Revolt

Sometimes in the day the blinds crack open,

then I can see a sliver of the outside:

some sun   a palm trees' crown   cloud bits.

My wife is selling our family home.

If anything should happen to me, have

compassion. She thinks

I do not know, believing I've misplaced

my memories. I still see   Mama and the aunts

plaiting their wool hair, feel a spring push

against my back,   that old mattress we shared.

The upright piano whose teeth woke us

every morning,   I cannot   escape

my head. I sit rocking. Brother, I wait,

know we are two fingers from the same hand. Come

see if I've pulled tufts of hair or dropped

my spoon like a baton on someone's head.

We need a new master—lock for the front gate;

tell no one   the combination. Plant

giant cacti with bold needles,   help me

out of this room,   it has been a long time

since someone touched my hand. At night—

        a low humming. I pat the songs we sang

on my lap, laugh a little to myself. Do you remember

where we hid candy? The Pilón coffee can.

It waits there with the letter I've written

to secure this birthright of ours. Brother, do not worry.

Our victory will be as brilliant as bite marks—

       those roses up and down my wife's arms.

Santo from the Sun

When the moon is full of lavender rings,
the Flamboyan's flames fall on the still street.
I follow the trail of rain that leads
inside your house. You carry my name:
Indio Solarei, Indio Solarei.
I mount you. Arch your back as I stretch out
in your skin, when my chest fills
with cigar smoke and my stomach tastes
the warmth of you—sweet rum. I sing.
The water rises from off the floor.
Sunflowers take root in my hands.
I pull your wrinkles smooth over your face.
Your wool hair hangs bone straight.
Cupping water, petals, seeds, river
stones in my hands, I rub your limbs,
soak your hair. Agua Florída anoints
our knees, and we move back and forth,
in sync with the drumming inside our body.
Your eyes are my eyes. We tilt our gaze up.
It feels like swimming, facing the fire opal sun.

The Visitor

I.
A row of crosses watch over this cemetery.
They are blue giants, their arms outstretched
and lined with blossoms–
the soul's fingerprints. The lavender sun sinks
gradually. These crosses approach
a cluster of graves
packed with a quiché lullaby,
covered in everyday doors of every color
except white. And some have knockers,
brass and lovely. And some are cracked and splintered,
ordinary and worn. We keep them company,
uncover each grave. We bring something good.
The pulp of fruit or honey bread,
a calabash, and our words
like the rain our dead drink.

II.
I do not imagine myself below
waiting for a visitor, a friend
in the shape of a sister, or listening
to the rain and remembering
that metallic sound it made
against the tin roof of the house I've left
in the backyards of my childhood.
But hope that when I pass, and you remove
the blue door from off of me
that your words are moist like rain. Will they make me
shudder the way a woman once did
in Chichicastenango, singing softly
ever so softly while braiding her daughter's hair?

Ours: El Naranjo de China

I return to our home
whose windows swung
out to the earth
we ate; the rim of light
casting African tulips
upon the cane.
I play the piano:
my fingers, keys
my feet, pedals.
I play the piano
until song tills
soil and the machete
no longer cuts
flesh. Awaken and rise
to take back our land
the miles and miles,
the sun that painted it
the orange of oranges.

Spirits Invade

My sister's leg keeps me
from turning, with one arm
tucked in, one arm draped
over my chest. And she falls
asleep with lips open
for spirits to invade,
draw a line down
the middle of her forehead,
so they can push water
from under her
eyelashes that look
like a moth's wet wing.
They force her mouth open
to reveal themselves
in whispers telling her
to dance, when our sheets
rise.

Slapping Bones

For Julian Ramirez

In a house whose writer disappeared,
cluttered by clothes hangers,
pads he'd stitch into shoulder seams
& the roosters his boss nurtured
for the cockfights, he'd tell me stories
of el campo, where the Flamboyans
sat apart & cane stretched out for miles.
Backroads where you could breathe,
bachata's beat like a distant drum
leading you. The pain in those songs
felt good that last night we were innocent.
He made a cat a paper cup shirt.
I pushed the cuticles of his left foot,
cutting nails that'd snap—and—fly.
Frank Reyes sang *Vine a decirte adios*
when we took our dominos out,
smacked one after the other
on the concrete floor, looking out
for the double-six promising to come;
each black pip that stared us in the face.

Bonao

Your father's two wives were neighbors,
and friends. Your mother's wide toothed smile.
She smelled of talcum and sweat
when she kissed hello and asked how I was.
We spent those days lazy, bathing in that cold
river that smelled like the mountains;
a mosaic of shirts and pants and socks
drying on the river's rocks, beside women who sang.

We played dominoes. We drank rum. We walked.
You showed me your father's lands.
Somewhere, a bonfire burned.
People danced the palo; the clack of sticks
filled a darkness swollen with bodies.
I'll die here, you told me.

There was your mother's dirt floor. We slept
behind a bed sheet separating her from us.
I saw a flame tree through the window,
smelled the chickens and goats out back,
tucked mosquito netting beneath my thighs,
feet, and head, just like you told me to do;
no cockroaches and beetles crawled
inside my ears. You said something about needing
to study, but the city, you did not miss it.

Near dawn, your father held your mother. His food
cold on the table. Your soft snoring
next to your mother's soft grunts. Your father's
Querida, Querida. In the morning,
you taught me how to knock a coconut down,
slice it so and take its milk.
Have you returned? Is the river still cold?
The ground that shade of red you could eat?

Surrogate Twin

After my twin, my next love was a kindergarten boy.
Lawrence with his white hair and white grin
as he stood in the corner peeking at me
as I peed to show him we were blood.
Our hands were the same size, though different
colors, and we fought like we liked running
or story books, or sticking our tongues out
at the girls who found it fun to collect clovers.
We told each other those things we keep—
if our twin sisters died, we'd die too,
and take all the maps in the map room to find
our souls. He may not remember
the way he traced my hand forever,
or how I said God gave the teacher's aide cancer.
I wish I could say, last I heard, my buddy Lawrence . . .
but truth is, the day before he moved,
he held a clip knife to my neck, then leaned in,
put his warm forehead against me.
We were six or seven. A dusky afternoon.
A long silence before we both took a breath.

At Home in the Modelo Market

An old man pulls the wrinkles of his dark face back.
I'm badder than you,
he tells me, handing me my change
for the rooster. My black & white
speckled rooster: My amulet,
like a necklace of herbs, I never told my mother about.

This market of rooms like those in a hive
or in one's head. Black bodies mark these walls,
& walk away into an amber countryside.
Then, a dark sun.
My father's black face he hated—the cobalt suit
he always wore, hanging here, in one of these rooms.

There is a woman and her baby;
a knee bobbing.
Buy a potion for luck, an elixir for love, she asks.
My father had a baby, a boy
whose name I learned in a letter
tucked in a book on Papa's shelf.

A faceless doll releases a bird—
one thousand pin pricks on the ear.
My mother was a saint who never said a word.
There are women plaiting hair
who only hear the way
hair sizzles & burns to seal the braids. Above,

wind chimes with full skirts & tiny brass legs
never stop ringing.
There was a time I believed
my family was dead
because I slipped that letter right back in its hiding place.
The saints in Mamajuana bottles.

It gives the rum a good kick.
An amber countryside
stretches across my eyes.
Then a baby falls to the ground. A Mosaic
of broken beaks & limbs at my feet & footsteps
never stop invading. Everyone needs a rooster.
They know how to keep the hens in line.

Child of Yemaya

Wizard Beach.
Foam skirts spread.
Your tentacles wrap
my waist. Yemaya,
you pull me farther out;
a thrust of your hips
throws steel-blue walls
over my head. I resist
your cold belly cradle.
I call on my ancestors
guarding Belie Belcan.
I see the moon: a little
white orb in your tides.
And *la nada*'s indigo
night falling all around.
Your frigid grasp.
A surfboard slices water.
Before a boy snatches
my hair, you push
a black pearl beneath
my tongue. You say:
*You have no right
to be mad.* My lungs
feel a great rush. Now,
I lie awake sleeping,
conch shells around
my neck hold your voice.
Your silhouette leans in.
And I hear the whisper
of my name. But I do not
answer. Even when shells
break against my neck.
Even when the black pearl
rolls off the dresser.

Boca Chica Aguacero

Fists of water
        cold and startling
against all those bodies,
        brilliant and black and tan,
rushing the pale green ocean.
        The weight of your petite hips
draws eyes up your dress
        stretched with music.
Your small feet trampling the sand.
        A white hand slithers
down your mahogany thigh.
        Shoulders rock back and forth,
side to side.
        You cock your hips con tigeraje
at the man swiveling brugal,
        his insistent *venire*
qui.
        Hawking the belt at your waist,
he slaps a hairy arm
        round your frame. Your lips part
and your eyes hesitate–
        a wide glorious brown.
Then you walk towards the shore.
        He follows—silently, obediently.

Memo

"Aye Memo, pobre Memo," we sing,

burying oranges and mangos and grapes;

pulp coming undone in our fingers

that turn the bellies hid in the earth

around a mausoleum where he sleeps

beside his own head. And we sing,

sing to wake el Baron Samedi. The thump

of our knees against the dirt, calls the sigh

within our chests, as night and rum

shade the cemetery, and the trees crown sky,

stretching their arms out to lift el Baron

from up and out of the ground. Memo stirs

surrounded by seven wings. He remembers

how he lost his head for wanting

another man. El Baron rises, wearing his top hat,

his black suit; he presses against our chests

to groan heavy, groan rough, welcoming

Memo to walk through the sealed door, bend over

and trace his name engraved into the wall.

Moca—1981

The wind rolls a ball of hair on the ground,

beside the boy's head; an ant climbs the slope

of his nose, up to his eyes, coveting

the tissue exposed to the sun. Here,

someone pulled honey from out of its nest.

A gold band hugging his finger; its two letters

spell his name. Here, where the cane is a giant

with no eyes, gathering the sweetness left

in the marrow of this land, someone's robbed

the bees. No one calls his name,

in this field where there's no sugar.

Border Crosser...

name my country.
Lean in, whisper
syllables of soul.
Ask: *Sabes espanol?*
in your accent from
between the Cayman
Islands and Toronto.
Phenomena
like the Atlantic
yanking at my sides.
Ask, *Sabes Espanol?*
in your conspirator's tone—
draw a sunset
across my heart.
Lean in, whisper: Home
between Hispaniola
and a silver republic,
some amorphous landscape
under blue-lizard waves.
Ask *sabes espanol?*
And when I turn
to draw your face,
make me visible
in an alphabet
from nowhere
in the world.

The Art of Divination

On rooftops so warm beneath my feet, we burned
silver gum wrappers, watched how they broke up
into cups of tea, and took turns to divine our futures.

Washington Dominican Heights Republic

In your matchbox
apartments, cramped
between the good furniture
covered in plastic
& the kitchen,
where we danced
on your linoleum floors.
I was taught to dance
Santo Domingo style,
& it felt alright
being locked up
between your winter—
How damn cold you were—
& the Caribbean
within your walls.
My cousins would say
You're alright B
& it was enough
being in you, with them,
drinking Presidente beer,
listening to bucket thumps,
the claves' clicking of wood,
how the electric steel of a guitar rang,
until sounds hit us hard,
hard enough to send us back
to the island in you.

A Wrangling

Straw hats. Sunday shoes.
Round and round the low concrete wall,
the inside pit; we kneel or stand
as the gamecocks begin
their dance. A few tufts of feathers
beside our feet. There is the dirt and heat
sticking to the air, the shine of our shoes.
Slowly one rooster raises its arm, pivots on its foot.

I once knew a woman whose lips seemed to want
to take refuge further inside her face,
beneath her hooked nose like the birds she raised.
Modesta could have been my grandmother
by the way she talked with her eyes,
the birthmarks down and up
her round apple cheeks.
She liked to coo and the chickens listened.

A generator hums. A flash of beak
disappears into the gold cuff of a rooster's neck.
A smooth black arm waves in front of my face.
Bets are raised. But it is quiet in my head.
One rooster rushing up and up;
the other hurls it to the ground.
The pecking's staccato. Tail feathers:
A hundred black sickles slicing the air.

She'd hide it in the fold of her skirt; held to it tight
against her thigh. She stretched out
her other arm, snapped or rubbed her fingers,
made kissing sounds that drew the chickens close.
The old ones went first, that's how she chose,
and with one single swoop she'd bring the machete
clean across   a delicate   white   neck.

This isn't third world or underworld. You kill to eat, she'd say.

The prize fighter will sleep next to his owner's side.
Its owner will clear a spot on the bed.
He'll stroke its head, feel the comb cut off for the game.
But one rooster lies, cradled in two giant arms;
a finger moves back and forth
along   its limp   black   head.

Tonight, the adrenaline in its blood will give it a good taste.

Learning to Speak Spanglish

I missed the S not in Spanish
but Español. Somewhere

between my tongue and throat—
not a *miss you*,

but something missing
in the words I spoke.

My friend Jesús tells me
to return home, to speak soft-like,

like even when it's bad
it still sounds sweet.

So I roll my Rs, practice
my prepositions.

It isn't *para*, but *por*.
Tell myself not *mas mejor*,

but simply *better*,
to repeat my mother's,

sank you, sank you,
hold not my father's, *hermano*,

but his, *Oye* brother, beautiful
day, no? And my mouth is:

A collision of two alphabets
without teeth.

Papi's Santo

Papi painted our home red, green,
the colors of his saint, Belie Belcan–

his chlamys floating behind him
his sword pointing at our home.

The dark dark night sighed.
Plum colored blades hugged

those flowers Mami calls
thoughts outnumbering us.

And I opened the door
to a cricket's voice;

my brother's silhouette growing large
over the living room floor.

Our door, with its rouged face,
its large brass hand, never closed.

Instead it widened its hips
so we could both pass

into the night's arms,
under the dim lamppost light.

And when we arrived,
white spread on walls,

traced patterns on sterile tiles.
Like two enormous wings,

Belie stood grinning
behind Papi's hospital bed.

My father's silver hair shone
against his mahogany skin.

His santo's smile cut
like the florescent light shining down on us.

Brother Door

There are no hands tallying on the clock;
no train of interlocking gears pushing forth
when your palm slams hard, thrusting splinters
beneath the door to your room.
I gather pieces of glass, of mirror, imagine
your feet, the tiny silver blades in your soles, then look
through the keyhole of this door and another and another,
until I can see: the pink of your mouth,
two porcelain birds still on your tongue.
Remember, when we were little, and bathing
together traced mole constellations across our backs?
Tonight, I'll sleep at your door, rest at your feet.
Island lizards clawing the chipped white walls.

Baby Thoughts

At fourteen I still played with dolls.
If one, just one fell or remained far,
I felt I was a bad mother.
You joke we'll have ten or more.
I drew moustaches on those dolls
not wanting them. Your hand rubbing
my belly. *One day, no?* I'm glad
babies don't come from thoughts.
I had a doll whose shiny eye
popped out. I stuck it back in but
she hawked you no matter what.
I took her eye and hid secrets
in its socket. The boy in kindergarten
who touched *mi parte.*
My friend, Trina, her black boobies
bobbing during recess; the boys
pointing and laughing. All were
in there. I wish my dolls were like
la Pelada: raggedy, bald, lovely.
In the water I dunked her
to teach her how to swim
or survive. She slept beside me,
her cotton body soaked.
Everyone called her ugly
Bien fea esa pelada.
Somehow she could take it
unlike her sisters and brothers
all suffocating in a black sack
after Mama killed lice in my hair. All,
save her. We negotiate the years
we'll wait. You play with names.
You ask: *choose.* My people believe
one's name is their soul's sound.
Yes, one day, no? And I remember
my dolls—unblinking and silent.

What the Gods Don't Determine

Mama & Papa buy me a cross.
Shiny silver capsule of God

makes me feel grown.
Spring's first sun, a drizzle of rain

& we ride away from the cathedral,
ready to conserve our crosses & bones.

Then Papa tells me don't look,
a man running naked in the street.

A hand across my eyes doesn't keep me
from staring at that man's behind,

smooth and black like Papa's.
I don't hear the car horns or the woman

chasing after him. I hear the low humming
of the cathedral's walls, see that man

descend as the pigeons do
in colored light streaming down

from stained glass windows to the ground.
At night, I bathe with my mother.

She tells of nine different angels
I can't see, running my hand

over the white rolls of her stomach.
In a story book, I discover twelve more

Gods and not a single one looks like me.
They've told me I'm a mythological hybrid,

how my broad back misses its wings,
the pigtails I wear are two horns

to defend myself with, and if I go to sleep
two hooves will replace my feet.

Next to a picture of my parents,
where Mama's hand rests on Papa's wool hair,

as he looks into her green eyes,
I set my cross down on the dresser.

In a Café on Corrientes

All day Mami you unpacked
street names
through childhood
recollections,
and Buenos Aires grew
small like barrio Flores
where your house still sits
with wet floor boards
and closets that hold.
Your parent's divorce—
the scar under your chest.

The closets remembered
your mother, Mami,
spelled her name
in rubbing alcohol,
the kind she drank
when your father's birds
lay dead on wet floorboards—
broken beaks,
crooked wings.
When he went away.

Your youngest sister drew
mandalas in the air,
trying to solve labyrinths
your parents laid out.
The door to your house
with its glass fingers,
packed in her throat
makes her stutter to this day.

And it was I, not your brother
pulling the owl out
from inside your throat
on that day
when the walls of your house
collapsed; when we sat
drinking coffee on Corrientes.

The Bird Doctor

He had a backyard of cages; a green canopy stretched above.
There were birds from Indonesia & the Caribbean,
owls kept apart, said to turn into Lechusas,
terrible bird-witches come to claim souls. *Pedacitos de Fuego*
he named his favorites. These tiny red birds with baby-soft bosoms
rising, falling, red and more red the more they smacked the bars,
so they could break their own necks. Flightless birds,
his rheas were six feet tall; their necks long like a woman.
Mama shares her name with the Ketupi; its bright yellow breast,
sharp black beak, the three stripes down its head he'd follow
teasing ugly-bird ugly-bird. The woodpeckers pecking echoed,
red hooded heads striking and striking a tune he tapped
on the ground. He loved them all as though they were
my grandmother, stolen out of a nunnery; another bird
he could not keep. My grandfather's hands: White
like a hundred-year snow in Buenos Aires. Talking hands,
hands that pointed & probed & slid down the stems of grasses
& herbs. In the July winters Grandpa wore shorts, convinced
cold pushes one's body to produce more antibodies
for the lungs. He'd make salads of alfalfa for asthma,
prescribed clusters of purple country flowers, honey,
& a glass of cow's blood. Our given names can vanish.
The Bird Doctor, he was called, though lines running across
his palms never told his story. They were never thick or deep,
splintered or run off. An obituary tells of a patient
he saved: a man who lived to be eighty years old with half a lung.
But it does not end with "survived by."
Mama tells me his new wife had treated him well. I wish
I could say his home still had the same green shutters, the wire fencing
all around, the compost pile in the backyard stretching for miles.
But there wasn't a number on the door.
I've never found Grandpa's grave. When I return to his city,
I'll keep visiting every cemetery until I find his.
A piece of butcher paper on his gravestone. A piece of charcoal.
The rubbing of letters spelling his name. The epitaph. The date.
I'll tell him about summer, and we'll talk like before.

A pair of peach fuzzed canaries will be cupped in his hands.
His birds will come in a swarm right out of his sleeves & vest.
His hairy white legs will rise silently. Everything will smell
of the pine needles & grass he brings each time he walks
out of el campo. And on his shoulder, a toucan will sit.
Its yellow bill: A horn swooping towards and away from his face.

Pinched Nerve

He sits on the couch
watching evening news
in Spanish and French,
eating sweet dried fruits.
Then he massages the new scar
down the back of his neck.

I wait for him to rise,
warrior-like, to call me
Muñeca, to take my hand,
place it on his chest and declare:
Coño, ese es un merengue!

His heavy feet step lightly.
His arms are strong and firm,
leading me into the dining room
where Juan Luis Guerra sings,
Ojala que llueve café en el campo.

He turns me.
His palm guides my back,
tells me to trust the tension
in our hands. Look up, not watch
the shuffle of our feet, to move
my hips like his.

I put my arms around his waist,
rest my head on his chest. Hear:
Ojala que llueve café en el campo.
And feel his childhood butterflies
flow out of his mouth as he laughs.

He rises.
We dance together, like before;
a dance I won't have to play
on the family room piano

while he remembers
the pinched nerve, and moves
his hand in tempo
with the notes I play for him.

Snow on Port-au-Prince: A Dirge

Snow covers Port-au-Prince.
At dawn, you cover the trees, the eyelids and lips
of the sleeping and those who wait.
The neighborhood priest lies quietly; a mob fights
over him, over his arms fixed and crossed over
his chest. His purple mouth holds the names
of their dead. And the concrete crucifix still sits,
a black monument within the rubble. There will be
more bodies to burn and bury. This one is
one more. Don't be afraid of death, Anna sings.

Papa repeats Haitians have always had dignity.
They are not ashamed of being black
like most Dominicans. At dawn, Papa sits rocking
before the TV, *my god, my god,* as a boy
spreads his arms to the sun; his snow covered limbs.
The neighborhood priest lies quietly; a mob fights
for his soul. In the Caribbean we bury our dead
quickly, knowing coffins don't preserve a thing.
Don't be afraid of death, Anna sings.

Snow dust covers Port-au-Prince.
At Dawn, you cover us. You cover
our bodies and rest in our mouths. You cover
our babies. You cover our concrete castles
now fallen, and our streets. You bury
our playgrounds, and our children's children.
You bury the orange of the Flamboyan trees,
and all of the colors that are Haiti. And you cover
this holy man we cannot burn or bury,
and so we sing his name. Don't be afraid
of death, Anna sings and sings. Brothers,
the body is still, the soul in our mouths.

Sabine's Shaven Head

Your hair: jagged and crinkled like hibiscuses we pluck
to tear and throw above us. You finger the contour
of your lip, mouth *toothpaste*, punctuating Ts
crisp and hard against your teeth, as though learning
their sound all over again. *Here*, you tell me, patting
your head, *here* you can find him. I didn't know
about the smell wrapping this little half-island, loaded
with bodies no one knows where to burn, bury or bless.
I didn't know about the bodies piled high, and Papa
face up among them–until your, *Here*. Two walls
of our house remain, like an obelisk on the outskirts
of Port-au-Prince. But our father's head—a smear of red.
There are *no words*, you say, for the hours you dragged
Papa to any hospital left. You repeat *nothing, nothing*;
your teeth chattering the way his plum lips quivered,
forcing something of a prayer inside of you. *So small*
in the backseat, you whisper, braiding your hair.
The methodical movement of your hands is a shouting:
Papa, Papa, in each over and under. But he's there.
Six hours you held him. How to forget that relief
gliding down your head, like a razor.

Bayardo

There will be merengue at your wake,
sweet rum, the taste on your lips. When you rise
out of your casket, everyone will see
the shiny gold watch slipping off
your tiny wrist. You'll climb out to face
an orange sky, and leave behind
the smell of laundry soap,
the kind you brought to Luperon
every time your belly ached
because you had had too much.
The portable television waits. And papaya shakes
we can feed to a cat that begs; matted fur
soft against our feet. Everyone will say
your liver was the cause of your pain.
I will tell them it was that the moon had
a black face like your father,
how your bony spine creaked
beneath the weight of our dead,
the rocking of a rocking chair that once held
your mother's frame, and lucid eyes you stuffed
into pockets—the mementos you'd rub
remembering your heart.

Cierto

How Tío Bayardo's heart stopped,
dancing with his cardiologist.
The two weeks after.
Tío Orlando, his heart's contractions
slowing to a nothing, before his golf game.
The wheelchair holding Tío Danilo's body.
The doctor that has said, he has no idea
how my uncle is still living.
And Tío Miguelito, losing himself
to Alzheimers, as he calls his wife, Mamá.
My mother tells my father to go,
visit the friends he's left behind
in Brazil, thirty some years ago,
to *disfrutar* before he can no longer walk.
My father makes plans to return
to Brazil, to France, to all the places,
the old neighborhood sorceress said he'd see
as a man. Around the world, she predicted right.
My father had laughed, the way he laughs now
making plans with my mother.
But he remembers too, driving to the market,
the way we do every Friday. "Buenooo,
first it's the chair, then the bed, then…"
My mother says, *Cierto*, with the nod of her head.
I imagine my father walking after his death.
Opening his eye real big with his pointer finger
to whisper, "Ojo, daughter. Ojo."

#49, Calle 2 Norte, Ensanche Luperon

The Flamboyan's red petals draw
blinds open, watch
a lizard's tiny footprints claw
at the chipping white walls
at the faded portraits of the dead
whispering above an oil lamp run dry,
next to knitted table doilies
I'll never weave, and Saint Michael's sword.

Confined by thin paper bed sheets
tangled in and out of my legs
and pillows that hold my crown of hair,
I sink into the coffee, in the glycerin soap
a mop pushes beneath a door,
in a voice outside pedaling
avocadoes, pan de agua, mangos.

Then the rooster sticks his head in my throat,
thrashing its tiny skull about to cry.
I rise to confront the tin tub waiting;
A tub that holds my childhood
in its rusted spots, and sits
in the concrete backyard,
fenced off by broken glass.

A Place Among Azaleas

I.
Say your name,
Each syllable spells my name—
Home across the back of your teeth.

II.
I kiss your eyelids
before the morning walks,
before we remember
the owls tucked in our chests.

III.
Mama taught me family history.
Chords I play on a piano that survived
Trujillo On Earth, God in Heaven,
the Dirty War too.
Put a cup to your ear so you can see
the birds we've inherited:
broken beaks won't fall from your mouth,
home will feel like the thumb you push against
the top of your mouth.

IV.
When you sleep you pray. Sister,
I feel your arm around my waist,
your leg on my legs, then, only then
I sing your name sing your name.

V.
Everyone in our family dies of the heart, of memory.
I will stuff you full of our song.
And when you sleep it will never claim
your heart, but sit like magnolias
in mama's old tea kettles, beside your head.

VI.

An urn should always have a place among azaleas.

Promise, you will not sleep with me, tucked beneath your chin.

Quilt

For Lauren Simpson

An hour of incense. The censer swinging
then stilled over your mother tucked in a cedar box
no bigger than your hands. How do these things go?
I imagined her long face propped in her palm,
a butterfly rash like blush across her cheek.
The giant smile you've inherited.

I burn incense for my Mama, make her spin
in the smoke for protection; it is purple
from an African Violet—the color we wore
on that day we lowered your mother.
I lock away a word like Lupus,
massaging her joints too swollen to bend.

We drove; a single black line never disrupted.
The whole city mute to the boots beating
in our ears, the flap of the flag as it was held out,
folded and tucked, then folded and tucked
into itself. That island of cloth against your chest,
as you patted it again and again.

Mama wants to be cremated. After I scatter
her ashes, I'll play a milonga she likes to sing.
No boots, no 21 gun salute, perhaps no line of cars.
I'll raise her flag from the southern tip of this world,
raise it parallel to the ground, straighten it, fold it,
tuck it into itself.

A Mouthful

Mr. Phillips reminds me of El Loco
from the old neighborhood, except he has all his teeth
save one and likes to tell stories,
stories like how he once made three hundred dollars
singing old folk songs on a corner.

He says he can't taste a thing and
sci-fi books are good indicators of mental health.
Sometimes he remembers the family farm.
He misses the steel pail, the hint of salt
in fresh milk, how each time he cracked an egg open,
he found twins. He lets me looks at his things:
an old tooth, an ace of spades, the box that held his medal
of honor—says he wouldn't kill women and children.

There's a twitch in his eyes. His whole face sags
when he laughs one of those laughs
that rattles his shoulders, makes him cough
just a little. On winter nights he waits
in a small park. I call his name.
He says that all he wants is to go home.
Home. He keeps telling me
that if I have any sense,
I'll stay close to the roots that are mine.

Pharmacy Bar

Sitting in front of the pharmacy bar, he leans
his weight on the red countertop, one arm slung
over the top of his thigh, the other bumps
the stamp machine that promises to ring; tokens
he'll use to pay the paper angels singing carols
down at him. Below the florescent light cutting
the tiled floor, the boxes within boxes, the small
thing he feels when the cotton of his hat
sinks down on his ears. He looks to the right, wanting
to see his face in the display case, alongside
the tiny porcelain figurine of a dog—
to be that small, that contained.

Migrations

San Nicolas fluctuated between mentor, master. The more I travelled the stairs,
he levitated. The more I slid my finger along his goldstone frame, he'd say,
Ciónnnnnnn. Father said he was the heart of an old wooden triptych, flanked
by the ups and downs of the Atlantic. Once, I kissed this saint for Father,
placed him facing the sky on the stairs, listening to Mother play a waltz.
See, I was too small to return him to that spot faded under his weight.
See, I learned to move among men, the way I moved around this saint.
See, when Father's god-voice broke, it broke like the sea and made me
wet myself. I had to wear a silky *bombacha* up to my chest,
baby-blue bloomers belonging to queen-nanny, Reina, Reina
rocked me in her boat-like arms, Reina, with hair like dune grass.

And I should tell you that after Reina left, Father took to cooking
because Mother preferred the realm of river women and men who changed
their forms at will. But Father was raised by women with arms
like kneaded dough. So he started with spicy stews, and fruit shakes
from the island, mixed milk and orange juice to create *morir-soñando*.
At first, Mother drank them for us because he needed to learn how to translate
love into something edible. So, he baked whole-kernel-cornbread, and mashed
yucca topped with the bite of cheddar, and when he wanted us to taste *la isla*,
he sautéd *tostones*, simmered red beans, served breakfast for dinner, a version
of *Tres Golpes* made you impervious to a Virginia chill. See, he knew why one
sucks marrow from bone, knew knowing fullness and feeling full.

Today, men still make me retreat to a space that mutes Father's rage
over finding a San Nicolas I loved and desecrated. But I should explain
it wasn't only this but the shadow of his father, a man reduced to two
memories, shiny silver spectacles, a clean pressed suit—a man who never
fed my Father. Perhaps it was also learning to exist in *Trujillo* Kingdom,
a patriarch delirious on power and women and whitening. Or globetrotting,
then the smack of ordinary at home: his American kids, his wife
living in a palace of books and in the silences of her childhood.
And wondering: Will I always be *el malo*, the villain in this movie?
The weight of family makes Father retreat. Where Mother remains
taciturn, tracing shapeshifting *galipotes* in her texts, Father charges,

improvising monologues that epitomize *he has no hairs on his tongue.*
Then compassion or guilt brings him back to revise conversations where
he tries to get it right. And I should tell you it's more complicated than
I confide. Father cringes seeing me dance, lacking the grace of a Dominican
lady. Father speaks to me in English but keeps our language with my siblings.
Father won't read this poem, and still resents my marriage to an Argentine
Jewish fellow, a white man who will never fully know how I walk
through the world. But it isn't only what came after, what came before.
I'm still learning to beat Father's pain. I still move among my people
as though every utterance demands deliberation because every situation
is *delicado.* But I'd rather declare: I dream with my Father's silk hands,

his squash and mozzarella quiche, his spinach and gruyere *tarta* makes
your eyes close to remember. I'd rather you picture us walking
to the Metro, biting into our baguettes, and know that I felt him getting old
by the rhythm of his gait. Know, Father perfected a canon of recipes
that exclude meat, fed me tofu marinated in soy sauce, garlic cloves, drops
of sesame oil, a pinch of coriander because *even though you're a vegetarian,*
you have to eat. And this Sunday, the last Sunday of the month he's dedicated
to gnocchi. Know, I won't be there to savor the undercurrent of sweet
yellow onions or red wine, to bite plump baby tomatoes and peppers, all upon
little doughs of heaven. Know that he knows this. And yet Papi calls to tell me
he's cooked something special, something *only for you, my dearest, my dear.*

Bienvenida

Mami, when you move back to that house
in Santo Domingo, Aunt Luz will smile
twenty-seven times for every year you did not live
in it; she'll remember feeling santos crawl
into the back of her dress, how she said
you wouldn't rock or walk under that roof
for a very very long time. No one believed her.
Now the house waits. Whispering hinges
replaced. A glass door gazing out at the gold
Malecón. And a new living room couch

unlike the one our Buddha looks after.
How will the Bride on our wall hang
back in the country where she was born?
The malachite mask from what was Zaire,
unsettled after having finally felt home? The piano.
Mami, the piano whose lungs hold your father's voice?
I will get you a cat like the one you'd say looked
like a magnolia amongst your furniture. Canaries,
if the piano does not go. And I will paint you

a girl facing a cage full of birds to make you feel
home. When you leave, take the mustard vase whose gaucho
guards our sheet music. Take the rocking chair
we slept in. The faceless muñecas, the scarves wrapped
around their heads. And Moroccan tea
kettles that hold my paintbrushes now. And books
you call children. And take me. We will crawl underneath
your new bed, creaking with the weight of twenty-seven
years, and read the newspaper like you did when you were a little girl.

Substantia Nigra

An ambush of teeth until your smile
chips the concrete. If I concentrate hard enough
can I keep the earth from shifting beneath you?
The neurologist read your brain like an old engrave
of the brain, smooth like a caecilian.
He pointed to the twinned structure nestled in the mid-brain,
darker than its neighbors. "A beautiful brain," he remarked.
I cling to that *beautiful.* But now you've fallen
again and we're dancing upon the steps and I try to steady
my lips, to not cringe at the porcelain sound of teeth,
or touch the tender skin down the ridge of your nose, steady
my words when the red flower emerges from your lips.
Everything inside of me moves out because I can't make the world
stable and your hands shake and I lie to you so fear doesn't make you
frozen. You smile through the blood: Round-apple cheekbones,
Viking-angular jaw, eyes like the green of a South American parrot.
I want to smile back as though no one fell but I'm falling
I'm falling in a way I'll never rise from where my face landed
and you took it in your hands and asked: *You were scared, no?*
And you seize me and stop the dizzy—the rise and then crash,
the world tipped on its axis, the fear that you won't catch—
Your intimacy with the rough surface beneath my feet.

In Papa's Shoes

A string too short to tie
from the first pair of shoes
he wore: Black shoes,
no soles.

He tells me about the bridges
underneath one's toes,
how if not given the right foundation
each one moves in a wrong direction.

My father never shined shoes,
he repeats proudly, remembering
the teacher that taught him at night,
to protect him from taunting.

Inheritance is like the skin
of an orange, the way it coils
like people and places colliding
in a timeless moment. My feet

do not match. A bunion juts out
from my left. The right holds
microscopic screws under a scar
running the length of my big toe.

Papa says we leave this world
only with what we've got on.
Pick out some nice shoes,
good shoes, shoes that won't hurt.

Dominican Republic for Sale

We believe in objects. Tiny pebbles

smooth in the hand. Plastic and metal

pocket-sized talismans we rub for luck.

What if you believe in Cigua birds

never disappearing,

or that touching a mother's hand

can revive your belief in amulets,

as the god in a boy's eyes takes off your cross?

This country is one big stained glass window.

Each of us a faceless man with peacock feathers

on our backs; our extra pair of eyes preparing

to dodge the next grenade.

A Place Where No Birds Would Warn Us

Some nights make me remember
how good it felt walking
with no light through a backdoor.
I'd escape to play dominos,
hear my girlfriends' tales
of how lovers could make them feel
electric inside. I felt their words
spell the how in my chest, drinking
rum-heat, selecting stories to tell

my ghosts. The ocean's salt,
always. Citrus trees fanning above.
The tiny black bags full of trash
& insects phosphorescent at night.
The song: the city's rocking knees,
clothes swaying on cement rooftops,
fruit knocked down on lovers hidden
in alleys—not alleys, but hallways
leading into one another's rooms.

Now, the dead pull. More and more
blackouts in the old neighborhood.
I don't wear my necklace for the blade
that'll steal its chain. Broken glass
tops fences & so many have fled,
faraway, searching for what's theirs
in the world of Diaspora.
At night, electricity gives,
a flux of light, flux of darkness,
and the flame trees look for me.

Are the Clouds Really Moving?

Are the clouds really moving, Tía,
if a man hangs in Pepin Park?
I want to believe that all of us
see a man hang in Pepin Park,
see shoeshine like tats on his hands,
see hands holding more than shoes
perhaps a woman from Hispaniola,
a woman of Bayahibe Rose.

Are the clouds really moving, Tía,
if a man hangs in Pepin Park
if laws render brothers and sisters
stateless? You said: *Faith, Always.*
I want to have faith
the South and DR are not fingers
from the same hand,
not a father and son stitching borders
of sugar and blood
at the cost of men like Tulile
hanging in Ercilia Pepin Park.

Are the clouds really moving, Tía,
if Jacque Viau's ghost chants
Oh Mississippi?[1]
The landscape of a man hangs
over the island like a bodement,
clouds pass through Tulile.
Tía, if you call: *Llévame a la Gloria*
mañana a las nueve.[2]
I'll respond: *Que por el espacio*
caminan las nubes.[3]

---

1 Jacques Viau Renaud, "A un líder negro asesinado (To a Black Leader Assassinated)" (1963).
2 "Take me to Glory tomorrow at nine/ Provided that the clouds are moving," from
"Caminan las Nubes (The Clouds are Moving)," song featured in *Music from the Dominican
Republic: Vol. 2, The Island of Española,* 1976.
3 Ibid, "Caminan las Nubes (The Clouds are Moving)."

Mammatus clouds cover the island,
Blue-grey lobes the sun tries to pierce.
Someone has set the cat among the pigeons.
Call: Tomorrow at nine, take me
to heaven. I'll respond:
Provided that the clouds are moving
moving over Tulile's body in Pepin Park,
shoeshine like tats on his hands,
hands holding more than shoes,
holding a woman of Bayahibe Rose.

The Record Collection

He used to listen with his eyes closed,
a set of black fingers drumming
the tambora's open tone. How she
never spoke a word, when he'd hear a smack—

throb within the conga's hollow stomach,
ringing & ringing inside him. These records
remained off-limits, tucked on a shelf,
before he died.

La güira's scrape falling down
falling on each one of our thirty—some vertebrae.
The trombone's smooth buzzing
further out & out until he'd would raise his hand

to keep me quiet. How she swallowed
the stare I gave her, after I'd once tried to listen,
the way he would listen to records
remaining here, the needle never touching them.

Aurora

There's a field in Manassas
where flocks feast on Gouda
and croissants, slices of granny-
smiths, plump seedless grapes.
Sizzling patties, ringlets
of chorizos, sips of filtered water
or spirits licking lips, among
Confederate and Union soldiers.

I stare at the golden beetle hills
through hawk-yellow eyes. Aurora
stolen from Guinea, stolen
from a Spanish ship. Survives.
A pallid swift hovering
in a tobacco field, above
a white throat she's slit. She raises
her finger to mouth *pà—ja—ro.*
Then wipes the blade against
my pants and yanks my arm.
Birds drum drum my heart.

The horizon is a flood of emerald
trees, trees she promises will conspire
with us if we never stop running
among the laughter and chuckles,
the sighs, the dogs panting after us,
the uncorked, uncapped bottles,
gurgles and gulps of air I can't tell
if they're mine or hers. Over one hill,
over another into the ring
of insects and grass betraying us.

Make like you are dead, she tells me,
Then fly. You are of the clouds,
Apsara, and change your form
at will. We will make ourselves
into a harmattan, dust-laden wind
whipping anyone at our heels.

Nesting

Red-crested bird
whose feather tips are lime,
I leave your bosom today, although
you've fed me the sun's honey
from your own beak, planted
an orchard of Asian pears and persimmons.
In my hair grows the garden you nurtured
for my smile: bits of Japanese maples
and marigolds. Round my neck are your braids
of amethyst cornflowers and goldfields,
clinging onto my chest like Ribbonsnakes.
My mark of you: A broach of purple cone buds
and blue dashers so that others know I am from
your flight, that you gave me life in a field of
spring where a dozen or so poplars and oaks
provided the most verdant sea of shade.
To you, my beloved, I leave a feast
of grasshoppers and acorns, marinated
in blackberries, and a jade caterpillar,
I ambushed and killed swiftly.
All in your honor.

Holding Hands

For Federico Abramzon

Offer me childhood and I'll marry
your hand, all 189 millimeters
stretched across the small of my back.

The center of your palm: a world
I bring up to my mouth to eat.
Draw me an orange morning,

breakfast and a park bench,
a couple of alfajores
and your 27 bones of music

spelling my name in beats;
123 ligaments, each one a syllable
wrapping round my knuckles

until we are—a clenched fist
of blooming flowers and limbs.
This here is our universe. Its axis:

your thumb's nine muscles.
Every time you hold my hand,
you lift me like water.

Love Letter to an Afterlife

Start as a slow rocking into sunset.
Each piano key: a rising and falling like a lung.
Be music when it came easy and be Sundays.
Sundays for milongas, and the day we speak with our dead.

When the night comes like a woman letting down her hair,
be a confirmation: a royal flag calling the carnival—
where a throng of guloyas dance,
horns and tusks tearing open a childlike fervor
I'm chasing now.

Be Bonao's green. The low hush of the reeds,
the river nearby, the water slapping the rocks.
The indigo sky above the women
lunging backwards, throwing coins
and prayers, into the river snaking below.

Then be a cigua that leads me
to a field of poppies. Be the red splash
across those blossoms. The wind—like the flick
of a horse's tail—as I walk among those flowers
and there is nothing, nothing but flowers.

Acknowledgments

Grateful acknowledgment is made to the editors of the following publication, where the poems below appeared, sometimes in slightly different versions.

Alaska Quarterly Review: In a Café on Corrientes

Anamesa: Dominican Republic for Sale

Bellevue Literary Review: Miguel's Revolt, and Migrations

Borderlands: Texas Poetry Review: Elementary Education, Two Trees

Border Senses: Learning to Speak Spanglish

Burning Word: Pharmacy Bar, and Brother Door

Callaloo: They Say the Santos Sang through You

Caper Literary Journal: Moca—1981

The Caribbean Writer: The Lost Santos, Child of Yemaya

Cold Mountain Review: The Bird Doctor, Slapping Bones

Front Range: Holding Hands

Interrobang: Playing Rocky and Apollo

Karavan: Snow on Port-au-Prince: A Dirge, Surrogate Twin, The Lost Santos, The Visitor

Kweli Journal: At Home in the Modelo Market

Lengua: Santo from the Sun, Papi's Santo, Ours: El Naranjo de China

The Literary Review: At Home in the Modelo Market

Nimrod: Love Letter to an Afterlife

Palabra: A Magazine of Chicano & Latino Literary Art: Memo, Bienvenida

Pluck: The Girl Who Taught Me how to Scream, A Mouthful, Playing Rocky and Apollo

Poet Lore: My Barrio, A Place Where No Birds Would Warn Us

Pterodáctilo: Communion, Moca—1981

Puerto del Sol: Baby Thoughts

Quercus Review: Washington Dominican Heights Republic, The Record Collection

Sakura Review: Surrogate Twin

Saranac Review: Bonao, A Wrangling, In Papa's Shoes

Sin Fronteras: Cierto

Wasafiri: At Home in the Modelo Market, Snow on Port-au-Prince: A Dirge, The Visitor

Witness: Sabine's Shaven Head

Yellow Medicine Review: The Mirage

Gratitude to Anders Sjöbohm for resurrecting some of these poems through his translations, which appeared in *Karavan: Litterär Tidskrift Pa Resa Mellan Kulturer*. Appreciation is given to Virginia Polytechnic Institute and State University; American University; Pan African Literary Forum; Northern Virginia Community College; University of Maryland; University of Hartford; Literacy Council of Northern Virginia; Fabretto Children's Foundation; and the DC Spotlight Newspaper.

Thank you to the following individuals and families who have supported me in more ways than one: Jeffery Renard Allen; Dr. Anita Baksh; Matias Blanco and Juana Merlo; Jon Burton; Paolat de la Cruz; Kyle Dargan; Nikki Giovanni; Dr. Carlton E. Green; Ana Farach; Alexandra Garcia; Hector Gonzalez and Luz Mendoza; Carolyn Hernandez; Rosalpina (Pinita) Herrera and the Herrera/Reyes/Sanjines dynasty; the Familia-Peña family; Jesús Jiménez Rodríguez; Melissa McElhiney; the Medina-Cuevas family; Dr. Jeremy Metz; Ogonnaya Onyike; Tanya and Chance Parker; Julian Ramirez; Alfie Scarborough; Rion Amilcar Scott; Dr. Isis Semaj-Hall; Stewart Shaw; Lauren Amanda Simpson; and the Su Wong family.

I am indebted to my mentors for their generosity, wisdom, and friendship: Carl Bean; Dr. Merle Collins; Dr. Hope Eghagha; Edward Falco; Robert Henry Graham; Dr. Sheila Jelen; David Keplinger, E. Ethelbert Miller; Dr. Randy Ontiveros; and Wendy Thompson. A gigantic thank you to David Keplinger for critiquing multiple versions of these poems. Know: The Flamboyan's red petals are the spine of this collection. A special thank you to E. Ethelbert Miller, who played a major role in the reshaping of this collection. Ethelbert, thank you for being so warm and encouraging when we first met. Thank you for offering constructive criticism, lending an ear, and smiling your never-ending smile more than a decade later. Robert Henry Graham, love, you taught me to decipher light and shadow, to explore the evolution and power of an image, to play and find the flow. I am forever grateful to you.

To Diane Goettel and the Black Lawrence Press family. Thank you will never be enough.

Much love to my siblings Ali, Michel, and Patricia; my niece, Arielle; and my extended family in the Dominican Republic, Argentina, and the United States (those who are still here and those who have passed). All of you have been sources of inspiration and encouragement. A special thank you to Josefa Rivera Rincón, my ghost, and my cousin Pep, who told me to keep writing when we were kids.

To the wombat-thief, Federico D. Abramzon, who pounces on my corazón and steals my alma: Thank you, Fede, for loving me on Jupiter and Mars.

Gratitude to my parents, Guillermo Rivera and Maria del Carmen (Ketupi) Prosdocimi de Rivera. Papi and Mami, you were the first word weavers I wanted to emulate. Thank you for planting golden nuggets in my ears, pushing me so hard to create, and never never letting up.

Ines P. Rivera Prosdocimi is the author of the poetry collection, *Love Letter to an Afterlife* (Black Lawrence Press, 2018). Her work has appeared in *Bellevue Literary Review, Cold Mountain Review, Kweli, Nimrod, Poet Lore, Puerto de Sol, The Caribbean Writer, Wasafiri,* and *Witness.* She holds a Ph.D. in Comparative Literature from the University of Maryland and an M.F.A. in Creative Writing from American University. Currently, she is an Assistant Professor at the University of Hartford where she teaches literature.